THE TROJAN HORSE

By Gilly Cameron Cooper

Consultant: Dr. Nick Saunders,
University College London

WORLD ALMANAC® LIBRARY

Please visit our web site at   www.garethstevens.com
For a free color catalog describing World Almanac® Library's list of high-quality books, call 1-800-542-2595 (USA) or 1-800-387-3178 (Canada).
World Almanac® Library's fax 1-877-542-2596.

Library of Congress Cataloging-in-Publication Data available upon request from publisher. Fax (414) 336-0157 for the attention of the Publishing Records Department.

ISBN-13: 978-0-8368-7750-2 (lib. bdg.)
ISBN-13: 978-0-8368-8150-9 (softcover)

This North America edition first published in 2007 by
World Almanac® Library
An Imprint of Gareth Stevens Publishing
1 Reader's Digest Road
Pleasantville, NY 10570-7000 USA

This edition copyright © 2007 by World Almanac® Library. Original edition copyright © 2006 by ticktock Entertainment Ltd. First published in Great Britain in 2006 by ticktock Media Ltd.,Unit 2, Orchard Business Centre, North Farm Road, Tunbridge Wells, Kent, TN2 3XF

World Almanac® Library managing editor: Valerie J. Weber
World Almanac® Library editor: Leifa Butrick
World Almanac® Library art direction: Tammy West

Printed in the United States of America

2 3 4 5 6 7 8 9 10 10 09 08

CONTENTS

The world of the ancient Greeks was bound by the Mediterranean Sea and the rugged lands surrounding it. It was a place of dangerous winds and sudden storms. The ancient Greeks saw their lives as controlled by spirits of nature and the gods. They told myths about how the gods fought with each other and created the universe. These stories helped explain what caused natural events, such as lightning and earthquakes, and the fates of individuals.

The ancient Greeks believed that 12 gods and goddesses ruled over the world. The 10 gods and goddesses shown on the next page are the most important ones. Some of them appear in this myth.

The ancient Greek gods and goddesses looked and acted like human beings. They fell in love, were jealous and vain, and argued with each other. But unlike humans, they were immortal. They did not die but lived forever. They also had superhuman strength and specific magical powers. Each god or goddess controlled certain forces of nature or aspects of human life, such as marriage or hunting.

In the myths, the gods had their favorite humans. Sometimes, the gods even had children with these people. Their children were thus half gods.

They were usually mortal, which meant that they could die. It also meant that they had some special powers, too. When their human children were in trouble, the gods would help them.

The gods liked to meddle in human life and took sides with different people. The gods also liked to play tricks on humans. They did so for many reasons—because it was fun; because they would gain something; or because they wanted to get even with someone.

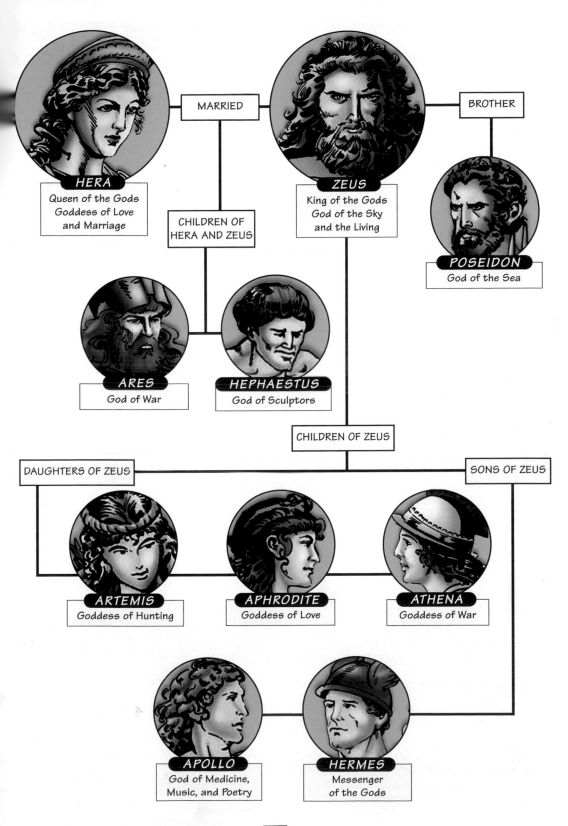

MARRIED

BROTHER

HERA
Queen of the Gods
Goddess of Love
and Marriage

ZEUS
King of the Gods
God of the Sky
and the Living

CHILDREN OF
HERA AND ZEUS

POSEIDON
God of the Sea

ARES
God of War

HEPHAESTUS
God of Sculptors

CHILDREN OF ZEUS

DAUGHTERS OF ZEUS

SONS OF ZEUS

ARTEMIS
Goddess of Hunting

APHRODITE
Goddess of Love

ATHENA
Goddess of War

APOLLO
God of Medicine,
Music, and Poetry

HERMES
Messenger
of the Gods

Three thousand years ago, Greece was not one big country. It was made up of many small kingdoms called city-states, such as Athens, Sparta, and Mycenae. Each city-state had its own leader. The most powerful was Agamemnon, king of Mycenae.

The Myceneans controlled some of the most important trade routes in the Mediterranean Sea. This control gave them power over other tribes and city-states throughout Greece. If Agamemnon ordered other tribes to fight for him, they had to do it. The Trojans were different because they were a wealthy, independent nation. They controlled many important trade routes from their great city, Troy. The Trojans and the Mycenean Greeks were rivals for many years before our story starts.

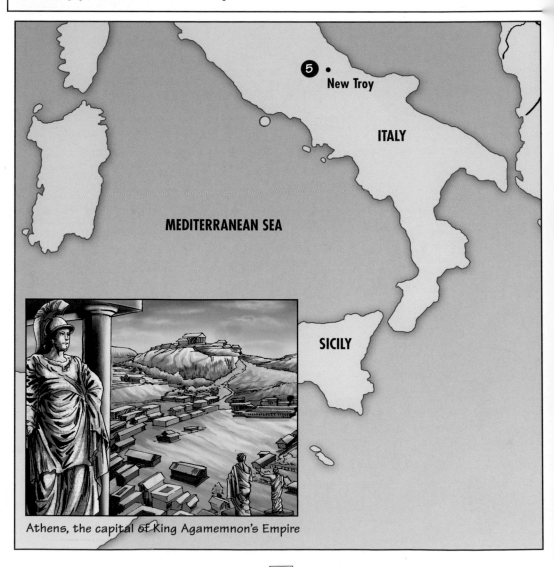

⑤ •
New Troy

ITALY

MEDITERRANEAN SEA

SICILY

Athens, the capital of King Agamemnon's Empire

KEY

1. Site of the Trojan War
2. Helen's and Menelaus's home
3. The island Menelaus's father lived on
4. The capital of King Agamemnon's Empire
5. The site of the new city of Troy
   Agamemnon's Empire

BLACK SEA

TURKEY

GREECE

AEGEAN SEA

1 • Troy

4 • Athens

Mycenae •

2 • Sparta

RHODES

CRETE **3** • Knossos

Hecuba, wife of King Priam of Troy, was pregnant. One night, she saw a blazing city in her dreams. An oracle told her, "This is a terrible sign. The child in your womb will ruin Troy. You must kill it!" When the baby was born, Priam gave it to his chief herdsman, Agelaus. The herdsman left the baby to die on Mount Ida, a hill overlooking Troy. When Agelaus returned a few days later, he found the baby alive and healthy. A wild bear had kept it alive.

Agelaus saw this as a sign that the child was meant to live. He decided to look after it. He called the baby Paris, and the boy grew up to be clever, strong, and very good-looking. He helped Agelaus look after his flocks. All the time, Paris had no idea that he was a prince of Troy.

The gods noticed Paris's good looks and bravery. At the same time, the mighty Zeus decided he was tired of hearing his wife, Hera, arguing with the goddesses Athena and Aphrodite. The three goddesses fought over which one of them was the most beautiful.

One day, the three goddesses visited Paris while he was herding his goats. "Zeus says you must give this golden apple to the most beautiful of the three of us," they announced. Paris wondered how he, an ordinary man, could possibly judge. One by one, the goddesses approached Paris. Each offered him a wonderful prize if he chose her. Hera went first.

Choose me. I'll make you lord of Asia and the richest man in the world.

Athena was next.

Choose me, and you will win every battle and be the wisest, most handsome man in the world.

Choose me, and I'll give you the love of Helen, the most beautiful woman who has ever lived.

Paris couldn't say no to Aphrodite's prize, but the other two were very upset. Muttering angrily, they decided to get revenge.

The most beautiful woman? Promise? All right. You win the golden apple.

Hera, we will make him pay for this!

Paris's life went back to normal. Then one day, he went to Troy to take part in the yearly games. He beat the king's sons at the boxing and running events. To save the family pride, two of the sons, Hector and Diephobus, challenged Paris to a fight. Agelaus was terrified that Paris would be killed and ran to King Priam.

Save him, King Priam. He is your son!

Paris was spared death and welcomed back as the long-lost prince.

Paris remembered Aphrodite's promise to give him Helen's love. He knew the famous beauty lived in Sparta and soon found an excuse to visit. He was welcomed in Sparta as an honored guest. Unfortunately, Helen had a husband, King Menelaus. The king was suddenly called away to his father's funeral in Crete. With Menelaus gone, Aphrodite began to work her magic on Paris and Helen.

Come back to Troy with me, Helen.

Hera, have mercy on me. I'm so in love, I'll have to go.

The night Menelaus left, Paris and Helen ran away together.

What have we done? May Aphrodite protect us!

Don't be frightened. My people will love you.

Menelaus was very angry. He stormed off to his brother Agamemnon, the most powerful king in Greece, to ask for his help.

Help me raise an army. This is an insult to us and the whole of Greece.

Hmmm, it is a good chance to add Troy to my empire.

Helen's beauty charmed the Trojans. King Priam swore never to let her go. But one day, Helen was gazing out to sea when she saw ships in the distance. She knew at once Menelaus had come to get her back. And he'd brought armies from all over Agememnon's empire.

What have I done? This face of mine has launched a thousand deadly ships against Troy.

DEADLOCK

Ten years had passed since Helen first saw those Greek ships on the horizon. All that time, the Greeks had camped outside the walls, blockading the city to make it surrender. Soldiers from both sides fought many small battles on the windy plains outside the walls, but no battle brought a complete victory and an end to the war. Brave warriors from both sides were killed.

The Greeks knew that the only way to beat the Trojans once and for all was to get over the city walls. But entering the city seemed impossible.

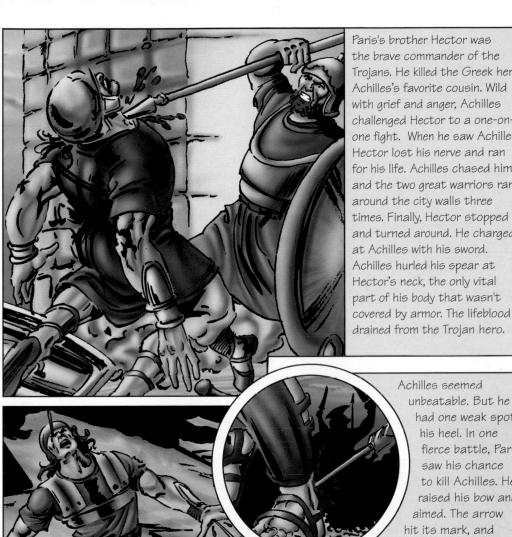

Paris's brother Hector was the brave commander of the Trojans. He killed the Greek hero Achilles's favorite cousin. Wild with grief and anger, Achilles challenged Hector to a one-on-one fight. When he saw Achilles. Hector lost his nerve and ran for his life. Achilles chased him, and the two great warriors ran around the city walls three times. Finally, Hector stopped and turned around. He charged at Achilles with his sword. Achilles hurled his spear at Hector's neck, the only vital part of his body that wasn't covered by armor. The lifeblood drained from the Trojan hero.

Achilles seemed unbeatable. But he had one weak spot, his heel. In one fierce battle, Paris saw his chance to kill Achilles. He raised his bow and aimed. The arrow hit its mark, and Achilles fell down, dead.

Paris was also doomed. The Greek warrior Philoctetes challenged him to an archery contest to the death. Paris didn't stand a chance. Although the first arrow went wide, the second pierced his hand, and the third blinded his right eye. But it was the fourth, which pierced Paris's ankle, that killed him. After his death, Helen was forced to marry Deiphobus, one of Paris's brothers. Still, the battle raged on between the Greeks and the Trojans.

The Greeks knew that the only way to beat the Trojans was to break down the thick walls that went around the city. But that seemed impossible.

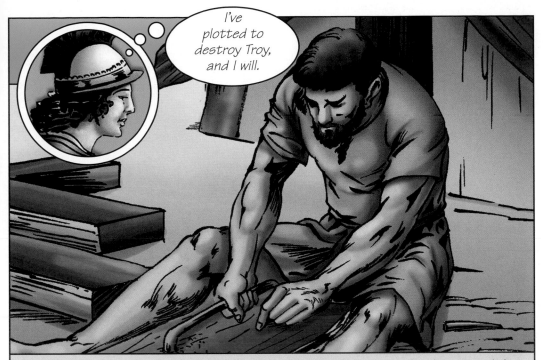

The gods were also tired of seeing so many people dying. Zeus held a council and suggested that the gods let Menelaus take Helen home without any more bloodshed. But Athena still wanted revenge because Paris hadn't chosen her as the most beautiful goddess. The council gave her one more chance. Athena looked down on the Greeks, wondering what she could do to finish the war. Her eyes fell on Epeius, a carpenter. He was carving animals, which gave her an idea.

Athena gave Epeius step-by-step instructions. First, she told Epeius to gather logs from the forest around the plain. Day after day, he cut down trees and made planks.

The Greek soldiers watched in amazement as a huge frame rose high above the camp. Then, Epeius laid planks over the framework and put in pegs to hold them in place.

Epeius and Athena finally finished their project. It was a giant wooden horse. High up underneath it, a trapdoor swung open to reveal a hollow belly, like an enormous cave.

Zeus, what on Earth is this? There's half a forest of trees in that thing!

Wow! What's it for? Is it a horse god?

ATHENA

For their return home, the Greeks give this offering of thanks.

Athena's last order to Epeius was to carve her name and a message on the side of the horse. Did the message mean the Greeks were going to give up the war and go home? And what was the trap door for?

One man knew exactly what it was for. He was Odysseus, a clever Greek who had been given instructions by Athena. Odysseus handpicked a group of the bravest Greek warriors. The group included Menelaus, who wanted to find Helen, and Neoptolemus, son of the mighty Achilles.

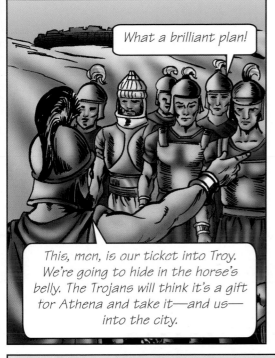

What a brilliant plan!

This, men, is our ticket into Troy. We're going to hide in the horse's belly. The Trojans will think it's a gift for Athena and take it—and us— into the city.

I made it. Why do I have to go?

Because, Epeius, you're the only one who knows how to work the trapdoor.

One by one, the warriors climbed into the belly of the horse. Epeius rolled up the ladder and shut the trapdoor. No one outside could see the door. The warriors sat in darkness, prepared for a long wait.

We will stick it out here until the rest pack up camp and sail off.

If the Trojans guess we're inside, we'll be in trouble.

Outside the horse, the Greek camp burst into activity. Following Odysseus's orders, the rest of the Greeks rolled up tents and bedding, packed away furniture, food, and animals, and loaded their ships. Soon, the only signs of the long war were scraps of litter swirling on the wind-blown plain and the giant wooden horse outlined against the sea.

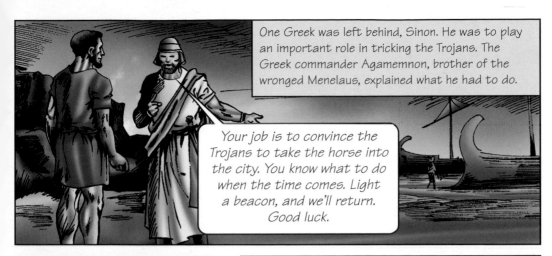

One Greek was left behind, Sinon. He was to play an important role in tricking the Trojans. The Greek commander Agamemnon, brother of the wronged Menelaus, explained what he had to do.

Your job is to convince the Trojans to take the horse into the city. You know what to do when the time comes. Light a beacon, and we'll return. Good luck.

The Greeks have gone! They've left something behind.

But the Greeks had not left at all. They had only sailed out of sight.

The Trojans thought that ten years of suffering were over. They poured out of the city gates. King Priam headed straight for the giant horse on the beach.

By Zeus, it's a giant horse. Maybe they left it behind because they couldn't get it on board.

Look at this mess!

19

The Trojans gathered around the wooden horse in amazement. Someone suggested making a hole to see what was inside. The priest, Laocoon, was sure it was a deadly trick and wanted to burn the horse. But King Priam saw the message to Athena carved into the horse's side.

Laocoon threw a spear at the horse with such force that the horse shook.

We'll be destroyed if we take it into our city. Burn it!

Thud!

Inside, the spear narrowly missed the head of Neoptolemus, son of Achilles, but he didn't move. Around him, other soldiers were sick with fear.

Excited cries interrupted these arguments about the horse. Shepherds pushed through the crowd and shoved a man onto the ground. It was Sinon, the Greek who had been left behind. He'd been taken prisoner. Little did the Trojans know that this was all part of the Greek plan.

Please protect me, King Priam. I knew terrible secrets about Odysseus, so he tried to kill me. But I managed to escape when they were packing up.

Priam set Sinon free—after he promised to explain why the Greeks had built the horse.

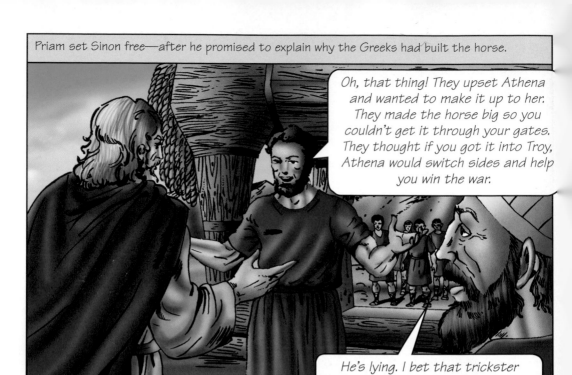

Oh, that thing! They upset Athena and wanted to make it up to her. They made the horse big so you couldn't get it through your gates. They thought if you got it into Troy, Athena would switch sides and help you win the war.

He's lying. I bet that trickster Odysseus told him to say all that.

Looking for help, Laocoon prayed to the sea god, Poseidon. But Poseidon had promised to help the Greeks. Suddenly, two giant sea serpents rose high above the crashing waves and headed straight for Laocoon's twin boys.

Poseidon, guide us!

Father! Look out!

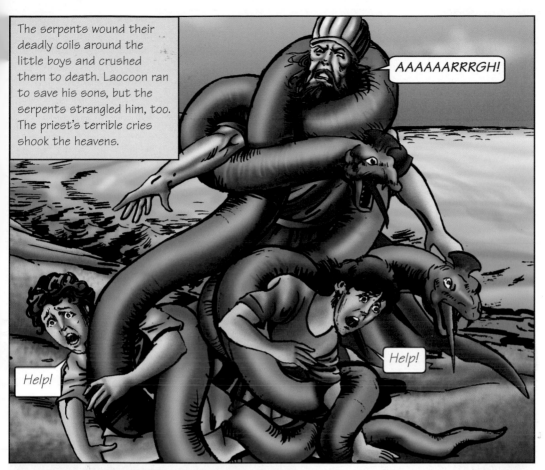

The serpents wound their deadly coils around the little boys and crushed them to death. Laocoon ran to save his sons, but the serpents strangled him, too. The priest's terrible cries shook the heavens.

AAAAAARRRGH!

Help!

Help!

The Trojans were horrified at the three deaths. They thought Athena had punished Laocoon for throwing a spear at the wooden horse. But they were wrong.

See, I was right. You've really upset Athena now.

Poor Laocoon! It seems you are right, Sinon. Take the wooden horse into the city right away. We'll honor it in Athena's name, and celebrate the end of the war.

TROY'S FATE IS SEALED

The horse was huge and very heavy. But the Trojan people put it onto a platform and placed logs underneath to roll it along. They slung rough ropes around its neck to pull it. Children and women followed, dancing, running, and laughing. As the horse moved forward, no one heard the clanking of the armor inside.

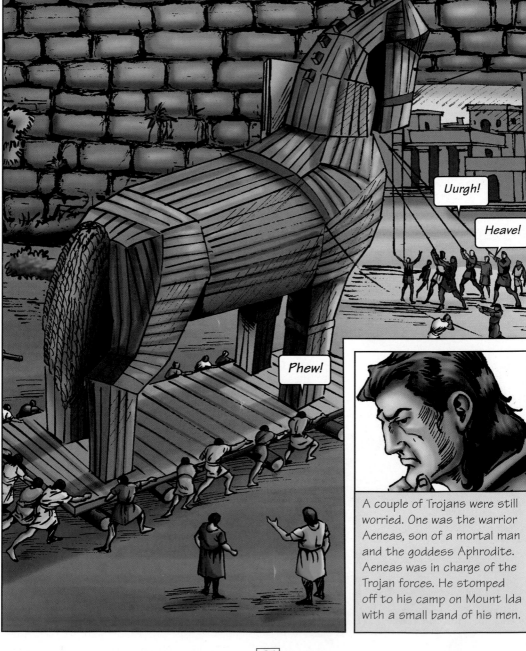

Uurgh!

Heave!

Phew!

A couple of Trojans were still worried. One was the warrior Aeneas, son of a mortal man and the goddess Aphrodite. Aeneas was in charge of the Trojan forces. He stomped off to his camp on Mount Ida with a small band of his men.

King Priam's daughter, Cassandra, could see into the future. She knew exactly what the Greeks were up to, but no one listened to her warnings.

You fools. That horse is full of armed men!

What is she talking about? Silly woman.

Finally, the horse was pulled to the center of the city, and the celebrations began. Roses were scattered around its feet. Golden daisies hung around the horse's neck. The townspeople danced, sang, drank, and feasted for the first time in ten long years. Inside the horse, the best of the Greek soldiers waited for their moment.

Hurrah!

Cheers! Praise to the goddess Athena!

Athena had heard Helen praying that she wanted to go home. So she told Helen about her plan and offered to help her return home.

As soon as she could, Helen left the party. She was excited at the thought of escaping from Troy.

Come on, Diephobus. Let's go and see the horse again.

If we must.

Good. The plan is working.

Helen walked around the horse, smiling to herself. She tapped its hollow legs. Helen knew the warriors inside could hear her and teased them by copying their wives' voices. Her husband, Diephobus, thought she was being funny.

What a fine horse you are! I think I'll call you Odysseus. Why do you stay away so long from me, your loving wife Penelope?

This is a silly game.

Inside the horse, the warriors were uncomfortable, nervous, and bored. Neoptolemus jumped when he thought he heard his wife call his name, and nearly shouted out in reply. Odysseus silenced him just in time.

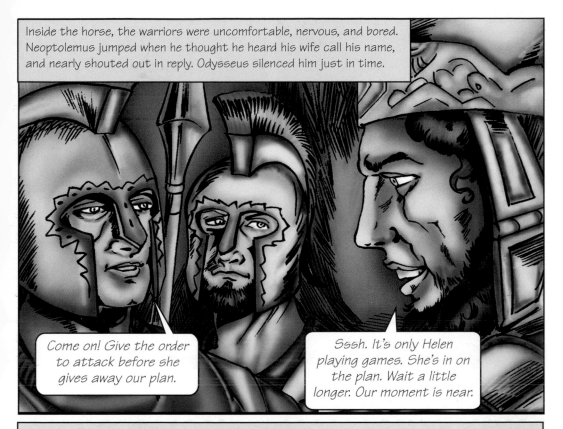

Come on! Give the order to attack before she gives away our plan.

Sssh. It's only Helen playing games. She's in on the plan. Wait a little longer. Our moment is near.

As night fell, Helen and Diephobus walked back to the palace. The streets were quiet. The only noises were the sounds of snoring. The townspeople had returned to their homes, happy and tired from partying. A couple of sentries remained on guard. But they dropped off to sleep.

At home, Helen lit a bowl of oil in her window. Now the Greeks would know where to find her.

At midnight, a full moon rose over the sea.

In the shining path of moonlight on the sea, the Greek fleet waited.

The Trojans had forgotten about Sinon. He slipped away from where he had been watching the party and headed for the city gates. He lifted the heavy bar, opened the gate, and went out.

This is almost too easy!

The fleet should be able to see this roaring fire.

Sinon gathered driftwood and made a bright fire.

Sinon raced back to the city and headed straight for the wooden horse, dodging the snoring sentries. He grabbed a rope and pulled himself up to the trapdoor. Back on shore, the Greek ships had landed. Hundreds of warriors were now advancing across the plain to the sleeping city.

Inside the horse, Epeius clicked open the secret trapdoor.

One by one, Greece's best soldiers climbed down their rope ladder onto the silent city streets.

You next.

Sssh, be quiet.

After their long wait, the Greek warriors were excited. The first in line couldn't wait any longer and jumped. But he'd forgotten how high the horse was and broke his neck when he landed.

Gasp!

Thud!

Their first job was to kill any sentries who might raise the alarm. The sentries were stabbed before they had time to wake up and realize what was happening.

The Greek armies were ready. The air around them was tight with tension. One of Odysseus's men ran to open the city gates. At Agamemnon's command, the army charged in, spears and swords drawn.

Charge! May Zeus give you courage! Let Troy BURN!

The Greek soldiers burst into houses and cut the throats of men lying helpless on their beds.

As soon as he heard the fighting, the Trojan commander Aeneas rushed into the city from his camp on Mount Ida. He saw the sleepy-eyed Trojans fighting desperately for their lives. The Greeks were killing the men without mercy. The soldiers dragged off women and children and made them prisoners.

They don't know what's hit them or how. We don't stand a chance.

Aeneas and his men joined the fight. Greek soldiers were everywhere, running through houses and streets. Then loud yells of triumph filled the air. In the smoke and flickering light of burning buildings, a group of Greek soldiers called to Aeneas and his men, mistaking them for fellow Greeks. They realized their mistake too late, and the Trojans murdered them. The Greeks' mistake gave one of Aeneas's soldiers an idea.

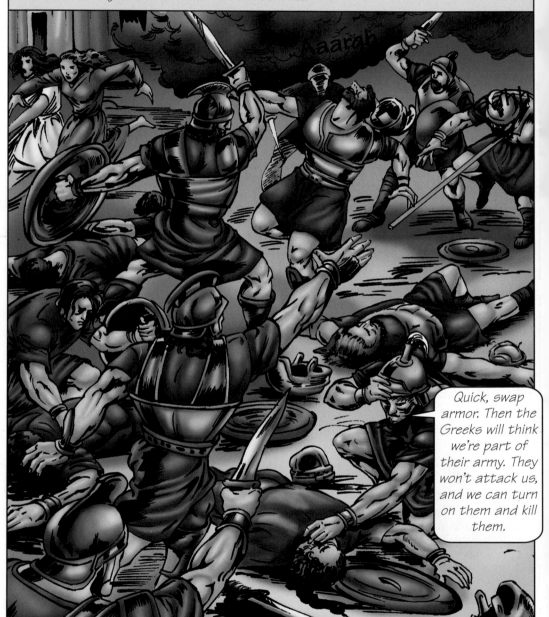

Quick, swap armor. Then the Greeks will think we're part of their army. They won't attack us, and we can turn on them and kill them.

Aeneas and his men ran through the streets, disguised in Greek armor. They won many bloody fights. It was the only time during that long night that the Trojans had the Greeks running for their lives. Some Greeks ran back to their ships. Others scrambled back up into the belly of the wooden horse.

Aeneas and his soldiers saw Priam's daughter, Cassandra, being dragged from a temple. Their disguise now turned against them. The Trojans on the temple roof fired a rain of deadly arrows at them.

Oh, by Zeus, they think we're Greeks!

Poseidon sat on a mountain and watched the battle.

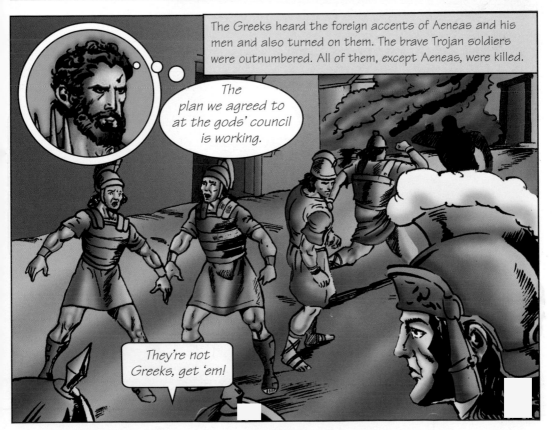

The Greeks heard the foreign accents of Aeneas and his men and also turned on them. The brave Trojan soldiers were outnumbered. All of them, except Aeneas, were killed.

The plan we agreed to at the gods' council is working.

They're not Greeks, get 'em!

In other parts of the city, the Trojans had run out of weapons. They tore up roof tiles and broke statues to throw at the Greeks. But the streets were full of Greeks. The Greek swords and spears flashed among the burning buildings.

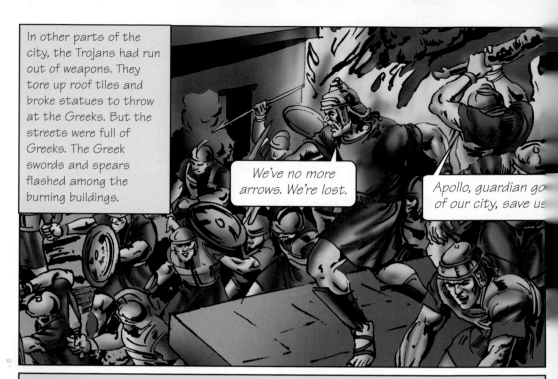

We've no more arrows. We're lost.

Apollo, guardian go of our city, save us

King Priam's wife, Queen Hecuba, fled to a safe place near the palace. There, beneath an ancient laurel tree, she gathered her daughters around her. King Priam put on the armor he had not worn for years, but it was too big for his old, wasted body.

Stay with us, old man. You're too weak to fight.

Maybe you're right. What can my old bones do?

Suddenly, there was a clash of metal and shouting. The royal couple watched in horror as their son ran toward them. He was followed by the Greek hero Neoptolemus, who stabbed him. Their son's blood gushed out over the altar steps. Priam threw his spear at Neoptolemus, but his throw was weak. The spearhead bounced off Neoptolemus's shield.

Neoptolemus grabbed Priam and pulled him to the edge of the palace. The old king's last sight was the blazing ruin of his city. Then Neoptolemus pushed his blade deep into the old man's body.

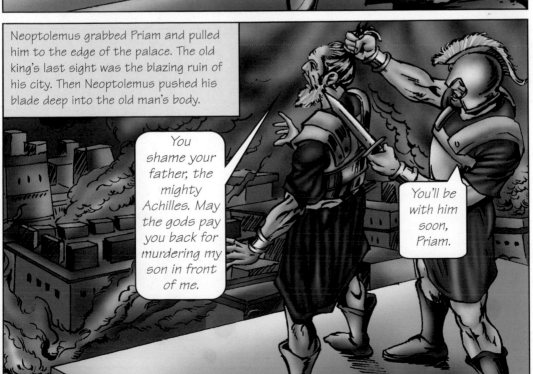

In the meantime, Aeneas stumbled home, along the ruined city streets. He saw Helen watching him from the palace and was filled with hatred and anger. But his mother, Aphrodite, spoke to him.

You! You are the curse of Troy. All this bloodshed, this terrible war, is your fault. You deserve to die. I will enjoy killing you.

Stop, my son. Don't waste your anger on this woman. Go to your father, your wife, and your little son and save them. It is not Helen's fault. It is the warring gods who are to blame.

Aphrodite guided Aeneas safely through the streets of Troy. On the way, she pointed out to him the work of the gods—the columns Poseidon destroyed with earthquakes and the storm clouds Athena had gathered. She also showed him Hera encouraging the Greek troops with battle cries. As Aphrodite promised, Aeneas's family and home were not harmed although everything around them blazed.

Come, we must escape.

What's the point of living now that Troy is dead? I'm an old man, I'd rather die here, fighting to the last.

What, run away? We should stand proud and defend our home to the last.

Just then, Aeneas's little boy's curly hair lit up as if with flames. It was a sign from the gods. On seeing it, Aeneas's family finally agreed to go with him.

Although the battle continued, all Menelaus wanted to do was to see Helen. He took Odysseus with him because Helen was bound to be closely guarded. High up, in the heart of the city, they saw a circle of light burning in a palace window. It was the fire that Helen had lit.

Menelaus couldn't believe his eyes. Helen had redeemed herself by stabbing Deipohobus. All thoughts of revenge drained from Menelaus's heart. He was once more charmed by Helen's spirit and beauty. He threw down his sword.

Zeus, what a woman! Helen!

Husband, forgive me. Will you take me home with you, where I belong?

Ten years of war had caused the deaths of countless brave men. Paris and an unfaithful wife had shamed him. But Menelaus forgave Helen all the same. In love once more, he led her gently to his ship. Helen was going home.

That's the woman we were fighting for.

Wow, she's gorgeous!

The battle was over. The last Trojans were defeated and removed from the palace. The Greeks gathered the treasure from the city. They took solid gold bowls and fine pottery, holy statues and beautifully made clothes. A Greek soldier guarded the long file of weeping women and children who were caught and would be used as slaves. Their husbands and fathers had all been killed.

The proud and ancient city of Troy was no more. Athena and Hera had their revenge on Paris for rejecting them at that beauty contest so long ago.

Now, it was time to even things out. The same gods who had helped the Greeks win the Trojan War would make them suffer now. It was the price they had to pay for victory. The first Greek to suffer was King Agamemnon. He took King Priam's daughter, Cassandra, as his wife. But when he returned home, his first wife, Clytemnestra, wasn't pleased. She murdered Agamemnon in his bath.

Odysseus also suffered. The gods made his return home very difficult. But that's another story . . . .

As for the Trojans, all was not lost. Aeneas led the Trojan people who were left through secret paths and tunnels beneath the city to Mount Ida. Once the Greeks finally left, the Trojans built a fleet of 20 ships. Apollo guided them to the east coast of Italy, where they built a new Troy. And the stories of the brave men who died for the good name of their city lived on in their hearts.

GLOSSARY

beacon *a fire lit as a signal*

fate *the future course of someone's life decided in advance by some supernatural force*

city-state *a village and surrounding lands or a big city with its own leader, laws, and government*

empire *a group of states ruled by a single king or queen*

fleet *a group of ships*

guardian god *a god that has a special responsibility for protecting a place or a person*

immortal *living forever, without dying. The gods are immortal.*

mortal *having a life that is ended by death, usually referring to humans as distinct from immortal gods*

myths *the stories of a tribe or people that tell of their gods, heroes, and turning points in their history*

offering *a gift made to a god as a thank you, such as a specially killed animal, or in the hope of winning the god's support*

oracle *a person who could see the future or explain the gods' wishes*

priest/priestess *a man or woman who devotes his or her life to serving the gods*

redeem *to release from blame*

revenge *to get even for something done wrong to a person*

rivals *two or more people who want the same thing when only one can have it*

sack *to attack, destroy, and rob a city or building*

sentry *a soldier who is keeping guard over a certain place*

superhuman *being stronger and smarter than a normal human*

trade route *a path along which people travel and buy or sell goods. Trade routes cross land and seas. Whoever controls a trade route can make a lot of money.*

tribute *a payment demanded by one city-state or country from another. It can be a punishment or a way for a powerful state to exert its power and make money from a weaker one.*

vain *being very proud of one's looks and skills*

BOOKS

Blood, Danielle. *15 Greek Myth Mini-Books.* New York: Instructor Books, 2001.

Clement-Davies, David. *Trojan Horse: The World's Greatest Adventure.* Eyewitness Readers (series) New York: DK Publishing, 1999.

Malam, John. *The Wooden Horse of Troy.* Ancient Myths (series). Minneapolis: Picture Window Books, 2004.

Sutcliff, Rosemary. *Black Ships Before Troy: The Story of The Iliad.* London: Frances Lincoln, 2005.

WEB SITES

Royalty.nu—The Trojan War— History, Myth and Homer
www.royalty.nu/legends/Troy.html
Brief, clear description of the Trojan War

Trojan Horse: History for Kids
www.historyforkids.org/learn/greeks/ religion/myths/trojanhorse.htm

The Trojan War
www.classicsunveiled.com/mythnet/html/ trojan.html
More background information on the story of the Trojan War

Publisher's note to educators and parents: Our editors have carefully reviewed these Web sites to ensure that they are suitable for children. Many Web sites change frequently, however, and we cannot guarantee that a site's future contents will continue to meet our high standards of quality and educational value. Be advised that children should be closely supervised whenever they access the Internet.

INDEX